WUNDERKEYS®

PRIMER PIANO BOOK TWO

W9-DEL-223

PRIMER
BOOK TWO

WunderKeys Primer Piano Book Two by Andrea and Trevor Dow
Copyright © 2017 Teach Music Today Learning Solutions
www.teachpianotoday.com and www.wunderkeys.com

An Introduction To WunderKeys

When I left home for college many years ago, I took with me a trunkful of clothes, a few pairs of shoes, a blanket, a pillow, and my favorite book, *Harold and the Purple Crayon*.

The book was torn, tattered, and loved to death.

As a young child, I needed my parents' help to cross the street or tie my shoes, but when I flipped through the pages of *Harold and the Purple Crayon*, I entered a world of inspiring adventures where I could do anything and be anyone.

So when I created WunderKeys with my husband, Trevor, we did so with one overriding goal in mind: to produce **piano method books** that would one day be packed into the trunk of a car – torn, tattered, and loved to death by a lifelong music student starting out on a new adventure.

Thank you for taking your piano students on our "wunderful" journey through music.

Andrea and Trevor Dow

Primer 2

Jam packed with age-appropriate piano pieces, off-the-bench activities, and game-based learning, WunderKeys Primer Piano Book 2 reinforces keyboard awareness and early note reading in an environment carefully crafted to meet the physical capabilities of young piano students. The book's engaging illustrations, hilarious dialogue, and step-by-step scaffolding approach combine to create the resource that piano teachers, piano parents, and piano students have been waiting for. In WunderKeys Primer Piano Book 2, students will:

1. Continue an exploration of the keyboard
2. Build hand strength and coordination
3. Identify notes on the grand staff using guide notes
4. Explore stepping and skipping notes
5. Use finger-number clues to identify starting positions
6. Read rhythmic notation and strengthen aural awareness
7. Begin to acquire confidence playing "out of position"

Note: The story-based instructions in this book are intended to be read aloud.

Hi, Sheldon. Hanging out with the birds this morning?

I start my day on the lines. I can see the walnut trees from up there.

That's great to hear, Sheldon, because today we're going to learn about some special line notes. Would you like to join us?

Wunder Notes are easy to recognize on the staff. Middle C is a Wunder Note! Another Wunder Note is Treble G.

Treble G is on the second line of the treble staff. Trace along the second line of the staff below, from the curl of the treble clef to the double bar line. How many Gs did your line touch? With your hands in Middle C Position, play the piece below.

Highline Hangout

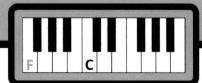

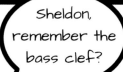

Sheldon, remember the bass clef?

Yes! It looks like my tail.

Sheldon's tail looks like a bass clef!

The ball of the bass clef sits on the fourth line of the bass staff. This is where you will find another **Wunder Note, Bass F**. Trace along the fourth line of the bass staff below. Count the Fs your line touched. With your hands in Middle C Position, play the piece.

5

Hey... my friends are on YOUR power lines now.

Ah, yes, I can see Gigi and Mr. Feathers!

You can play with them soon, but first join us as we play a game with the Wunder Notes.

Where Are The Wunder Notes?

Thanks for your help. Gotta fly!

My birdy buddies are gone!

Let's help Sheldon find <u>G</u>igi and Mr. <u>F</u>eathers.

I will place masking tape onto six coins. I will label three coins with the note name G (for Treble G) and three coins with the note name F (for Bass F). While your eyes are closed, I will hide the coins in the room. Next, I will draw a large grand staff on a piece of paper and place it on the floor. Now search the room for the coins. When you find one, use its labeled note name to **place it on the grand staff** in its correct position. Keep playing until all six coins are on the grand staff.

In the music below, can you point to a practice piece that is played softly? Loudly?

Use your RH 5 to tap all the Treble Gs. Use your LH 5 to tap all the Bass Fs.

Place your hands in Middle C Position. I will point to a note below. Play its matching key.

Practice On The Pathway

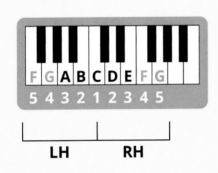

LH   **RH**

Listen as I clap the rhythms of the practice pieces. Can you clap the rhythms back to me?

Listen and watch as I play each practice piece.

Now it's your turn. Place your hands in Middle C Position. Play each practice piece. Say the note names as you play.

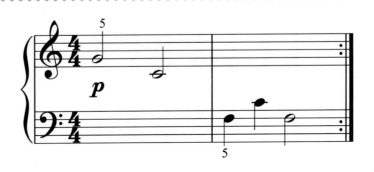

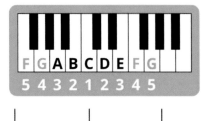

A Treetop Tune

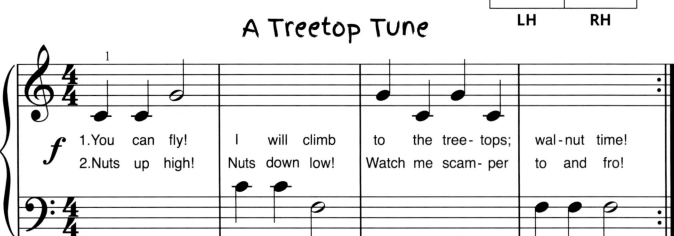

1. You can fly! I will climb to the tree-tops; wal-nut time!
2. Nuts up high! Nuts down low! Watch me scam-per to and fro!

The Walnut Waltz

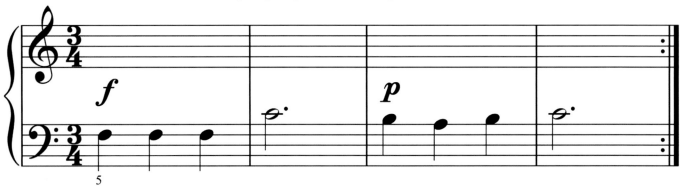

Tightrope Walker

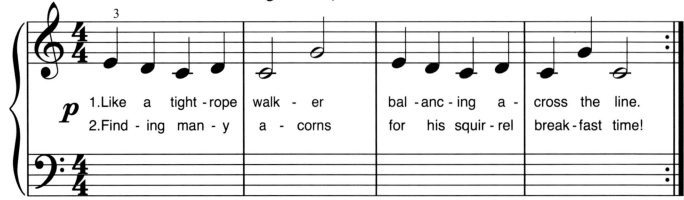

1. Like a tight-rope walk-er bal-anc-ing a-cross the line.
2. Find-ing man-y a-corns for his squir-rel break-fast time!

Feathered Friends

1.Pit - ter, pat - ter | from the sky. | Who's there in the | tree - top?
2.Shel- don and his | feath-ered friends | mak - ing all the | nuts drop!

Scurry Up

Highline Hangout

1. Let's help Sheldon bring color back to Chirp, Gigi, and Mr. Feathers.

2. Look at each measure below. If the note on the staff is Bass F, color the corresponding bird **blue**. If the note on the staff is Middle C, color the corresponding bird **red**. If the note on the staff is Treble G, color the corresponding bird **green**.

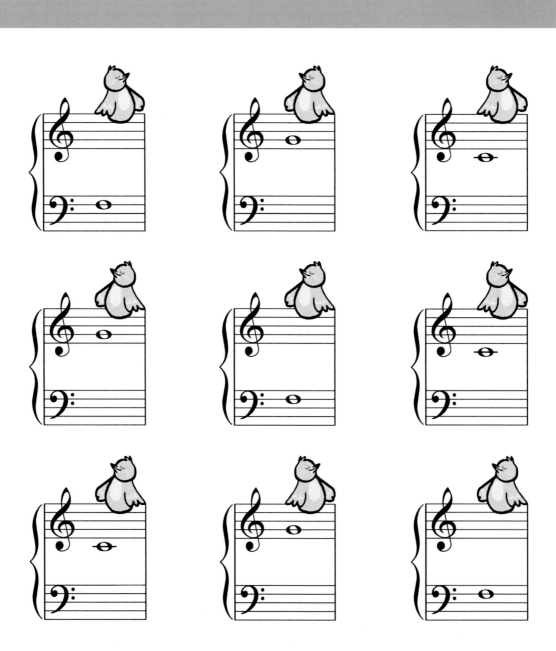

Playing With Stacked Notes

1 When notes on the staff are placed on top of each other, they are **played at the same time**. Look at the music to the right. Name the Wunder Notes in each stack.

2 Place your hands in Middle C Position. Using your RH 1 and 5 fingers and your LH 5 and 1 fingers, practice playing the stacked notes.

Cool Cousins

Gary, please put Larry down.

Look out! Grizzlies on the go!

Playing With Stacked Notes

1. While Gary puts Larry down, let's practice playing with stacked notes.

2. Place your hands in Middle C Position and listen as I clap a simple rhythm.

3. **Can you play the rhythm back** to me using your RH 1 and 5 to play Middle C and Treble G together? Try again, using your LH 5 and 1 to play Bass F and Middle C together.

Phew! What is that awful smell?

Larry packed fish for the penguins. It must be thawing.

FISH! Gary, I think it's time for the two of you to go, but before you do, let's play a quick game.

Piggybacking Penguins

When we play stacked notes on the piano, we hear two pitches at the same time. **Let's play a listening game.**

I will draw a large iceberg on a piece of paper. Place ten coins (penguins) in the "water" around the iceberg. I will play a single note or a pair of stacked notes on the piano. If you hear one pitch (a single note), place one penguin on the iceberg. If you hear two pitches (stacked notes), **stack two coins** on top of each other and then place them on the iceberg. Let's play until all the coins are on the iceberg.

Keep it cool! We've got to run!

Cool Cousins

Point to the stacked notes that are played with your right hand.

Point to the stacked notes that are played with your left hand.

Place your hands in Middle C Position. I will point to a note(s). Play the matching key(s).

Practice On The Pathway

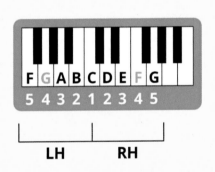

Listen as I clap the rhythms of the practice pieces. Can you clap the rhythms back to me?

Listen and watch as I play each practice piece.

Now it's your turn. Place your hands in Middle C Position. Play each practice piece.

Did you remember to play the first piece loudly? The last piece softly?

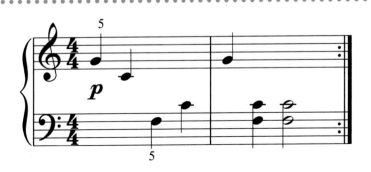

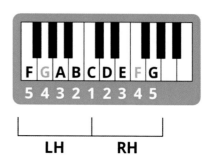

LH   RH

Through The Snow

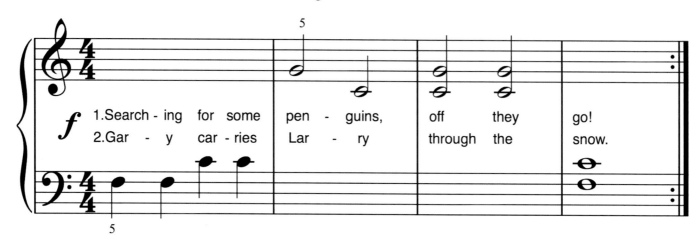

Keep It Cool

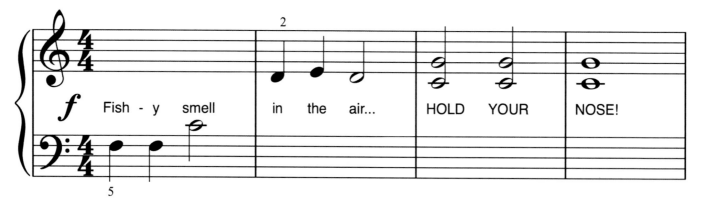

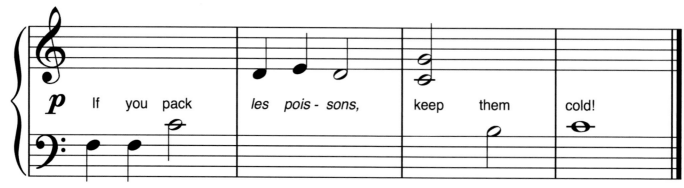

Note: The playing cards for *Cool Cousins* are found at the end of this book.

Players: two players   **Materials:**   one laminated game board, ten playing cards, nine pennies, nine dimes, two dice

Game Objectives:

Musical Objective: To reinforce recognition of Bass F, Middle C, and Treble G
Game Objective: To place more coins over iceberg images than an opposing player

Setting It Up:

Players should sit beside one another with the game board placed in front and the deck of cards placed to the side. Player 1 should have a die and nine pennies. Player 2 should have a die and nine dimes.

How To Play:

1. To begin, either player removes the top card from the deck and flips it over to reveal an image of a note on the grand staff accompanied by a number.

2. At this point the game becomes a race, with each player rolling her die in an attempt to have it display a value that corresponds to the number revealed on the card in Step 1. The first player to roll the matching value wins the round.

3. The player winning the round names the note on the card revealed in Step 1 and places one coin over any iceberg image on the game board displaying a note name that matches the note image on the card.

4. Players repeat Steps 1 to 3 until all cards have been removed from the deck.

5. At this point the game is over and the player with the most coins on the game board wins the game.

Starving For Skips

On the music staff, a skip occurs when a line note immediately follows a line note or a space note immediately follows a space note. A step occurs when a line note immediately follows a space note or a space note immediately follows a line note. Inside the circles below are stepping notes and skipping notes. Draw a line from each circle of **skipping notes** to the shark.

Surf's Up Skunk

If so, I think I'll skip surfing.

Are there sharks in the ocean?

Since Maxine's going to skip surfing, let's skip on the keyboard instead. **I will place four dice** (sharks) on white keys. Choose any die on the keyboard. Use your RH 1 to play the white key immediately below the die and your RH 3 to play the white key immediately above the die. **You just played a skip!** Use your RH 1 and 3 to skip over the remaining sharks (dice). Can you play again using your LH 3 and 1? RH 3 and 5? LH 5 and 3?

Maxine, you did well skipping over the sharks. Are you sure you don't want to go surfing?

I think I'm feeling brave enough to ride the waves.

Well, before you paddle away, grab a pencil and join us as we explore skipping on line notes.

Skipping On Line Notes

We'll practice skipping on space notes in later lessons, but for now **let's practice skipping** on line notes. Wunder Notes Bass F, Middle C, and Treble G are line notes. Treble E and Bass A are also line notes. Look at the two music staves to the right.

A shark has eaten the notes! On each staff draw the correct notes above their note names. Next, with your hands in Middle C Position, practice skipping on the treble staff and then on the bass staff.

Can you find notes in the practice pieces below that are skipping up? Skipping down?

Use your LH 5 to tap all the Bass Fs. Use your RH 5 to tap all the Treble Gs.

Place your hands in Middle C Position. I will point to a note below. Play its matching key.

Practice On The Pathway

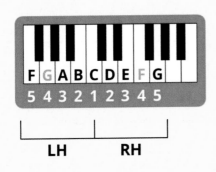

Listen as I clap the rhythms of the practice pieces. Can you clap the rhythms back to me?

Listen and watch as I play each practice piece.

Now it's your turn. Place your hands in Middle C Position. Play each practice piece. Say the note names as you play.

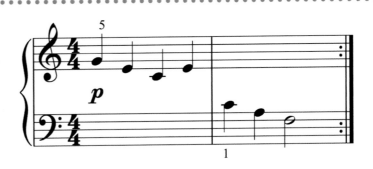

Surf's Up Skunk

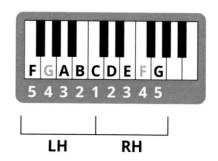

Hang Ten

Surf - ing | on the o - cean! | Hang ten | on the waves!

Max - ine's | hav - ing fun and | feel - ing | brave!

Wave Skipper

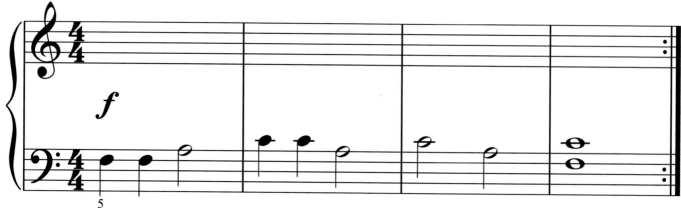

Surf's Up!

A Toothy Tune

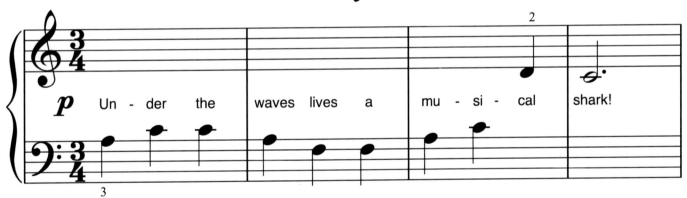

Un - der the waves lives a mu - si - cal shark!

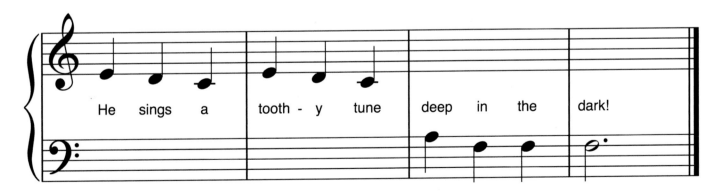

He sings a tooth - y tune deep in the dark!

Surf's Up Skunk

1. **I will read to you** the statement in the first box below. If your answer to the statement is "yes," draw a note on the measure of music that is a skip above the existing note.

2. If your answer to the statement is "no," draw a note on the measure of music that is a step above the existing note. Let's keep playing!

 I have been on a boat.

 I have built a sandcastle.

 I have been pinched by a crab.

 I like to eat fish.

 I know how to swim.

Ah, Ruby. I see you've found your way into my garden.

I must say, your harvest is especially delicious this year.

I chose the "extra crunchy" carrot seeds just for you. Now finish chewing and join us as we learn to read F.

I know F already.

That was Bass F.

1. **Let's learn a new F!** Treble F is found in the first space on the treble staff. It is a step above E and a step below Wunder Note G. On the keyboard, F is found below a group of three black keys.

2. Point to Treble F on the staff to the right. With your hands in Middle C Position, practice stepping between E, F, and G.

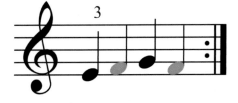

Gobble Up The Garden

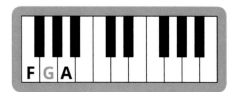

1. While Ruby dreams of greens, let's learn a new G. **Bass G is in the top space** on the bass staff. It is a step above Wunder Note F and a step below A. On the keyboard, G is one step higher than F.

2. Point to Bass G on the staff to the right. With your hands in Middle C Position, practice stepping between F, G, and A.

Note Crunching With Carrots

I will draw a large carrot on a piece of paper. Next, I will cut out four leaf-shaped slips of paper and label one E, one F, one G, and one A. Sit on the floor. I will point to a measure of music below. Find the leaves labeled with the note names that match the notes in the measure. Place them in order on the top of the carrot. Let's remove the leaves and play again.

Gobble Up The Garden

In the practice pieces below, use your RH 4 to tap all the Treble Fs.

In the practice pieces below, use your LH 4 to tap all the Bass Gs.

Place your hands in Middle C Position. I will point to a note below. Play its matching key.

Practice On The Pathway

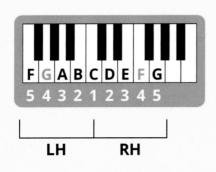

Listen as I clap the rhythms of the practice pieces. Can you clap the rhythms back to me?

Listen and watch as I play each practice piece.

Now it's your turn. Place your hands in Middle C Position. Play each practice piece. Say the note names as you play.

Gobble Up The Garden

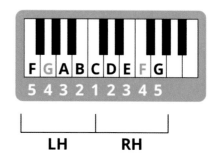

F G A B C D E F G
5 4 3 2 1 2 3 4 5

LH   RH

Leafy Greens

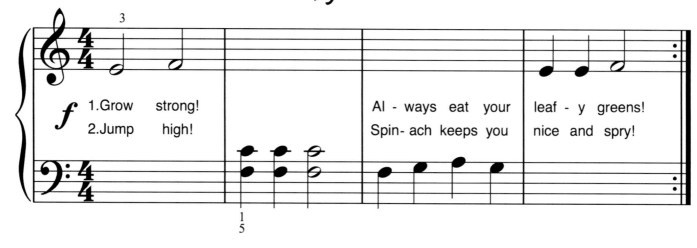

f
1.Grow   strong!
2.Jump   high!

Al - ways eat your
Spin- ach keeps you

leaf - y greens!
nice and spry!

Carrots In The Kitchen

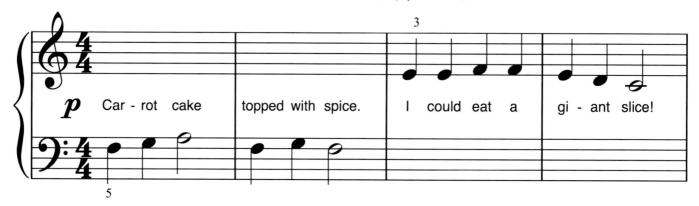

p   Car - rot cake   topped with spice.   I could eat a   gi - ant slice!

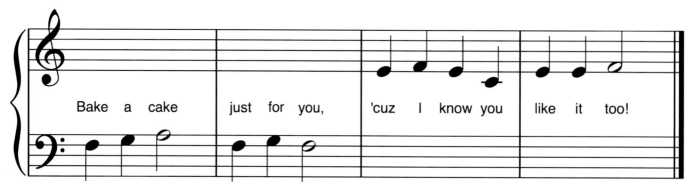

Bake a cake   just for you,   'cuz I know you   like it too!

R.H.

1.   2.

L.H.

Gobble Up The Garden

Note: The playing cards for *Gobble Up The Garden* are found at the end of this book.

Players: two players

Materials: one laminated game board, twelve coins, ten playing cards

Game Objectives:

Musical Objective: To reinforce recognition of Bass G and Treble F
Game Objective: To remove five coins before an opposing player

Setting It Up:

Players should sit beside one another with the game board placed in front and the deck of cards placed between. One coin should be placed over each of the twelve carrots, concealing the letter.

How To Play:

1. To begin, Player 1 removes the top card from the deck and flips it over to reveal an image of a note on the grand staff.

2. Player 1 determines the name of the note and then removes any coin from a carrot image on the game board.

3. If the letter revealed by the coin removed in Step 2 matches the note image on the back of the card selected in Step 1, Player 1 keeps the coin. If a match is not found, the coin is placed back on the carrot image on the game board.

4. The card selected in Step 1 is removed from the deck and then Player 2 repeats Steps 1 to 3.

5. Players continue alternating turns until one player removes five coins from the game board and wins the game.

6. If all cards have been removed from the deck and a player has not collected five coins, the cards are shuffled and play is continued.

I'm glad to see you, Sheldon, but it's Gary's lesson time.

Gary is hibernating. He said I should come instead.

Gary shouldn't hibernate until winter. Are you sure he isn't napping? Well, since Gary skipped his lesson, let's learn how to skip on space notes.

Skipping On Space Notes

I will write D-F on four slips of paper and G-B on four slips of paper and place them face down on the floor. Turn over one piece of paper. Read the note names and find the matching measure below. **Color a circle** on the side of Gary that is closest to the matching measure. Let's play until three circles on one side of Gary have been colored. Did Gary wake up or stay asleep?

Asleep   Awake

Bedtime Brouhaha

1. While Sheldon checks on Gary, let's play a game. **Stand on one side of the room.** I will place a "sleepy" stuffed animal (Gary!) on the other side of the room.

2. Listen to the skips I play on the piano. If the skips I play are moving higher, hop forward once. If the skips I play are moving lower, hop backward once.

3. Let's keep playing until you reach the stuffy!

Sheldon! Wait! Not a good idea. Let Gary wake up on his own. You stay here and join us as we have more fun with skipping.

Let's Skip On Space Notes

Place your hands in Middle C Position. **I will point to a measure.** If Gary is above the measure, play and say the notes *piano*. If Sheldon is above the measure, play and say the notes *forte*.

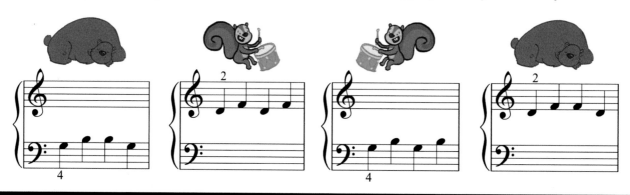

Look at the practice pieces below. Using a pencil, circle a skip between G and B, B and G, F and D, and finally, D and F.

Place your hands in Middle C Position. I will point to a note. Name the note then play its matching key.

Practice On The Pathway

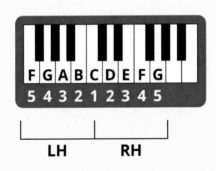

LH   RH

Listen as I clap the rhythms of the practice pieces. Can you clap the rhythms back to me?

Listen and watch as I play each practice piece.

Now it's your turn. Place your hands in Middle C Position. Play each practice piece. Say the note names as you play.

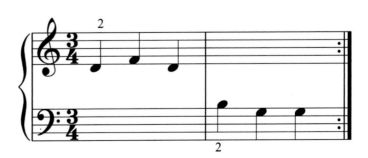

Bedtime Brouhaha

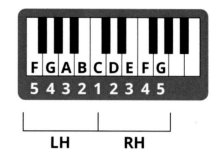

F G A B C D E F G
5 4 3 2 1 2 3 4 5

LH   RH

Sleeping 'Til Springtime

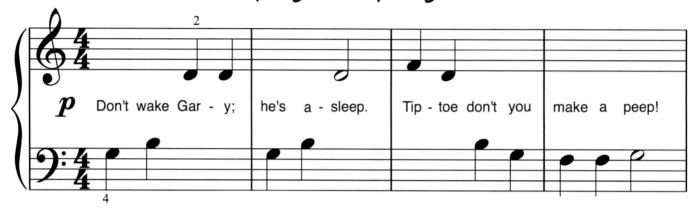

Don't wake Gar - y; he's a - sleep. Tip - toe don't you make a peep!

Don't play trum - pets! Don't bang drums! He will sleep 'til spring - time comes!

Bluesy Lullaby

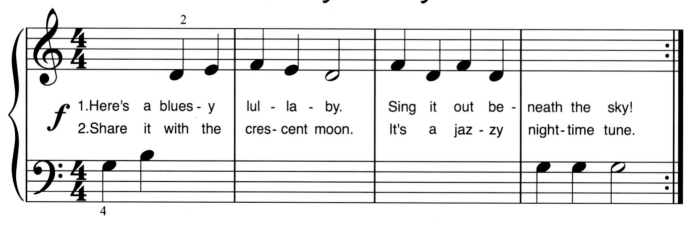

1. Here's a blues - y lul - la - by. Sing it out be - neath the sky!
2. Share it with the cres - cent moon. It's a jaz - zy night - time tune.

Gary, did you just land a hot air balloon in my yard?

Yup, it's moving day. I'm using the balloon to search for a new den.

You're always on the move, Gary! That's a good thing, because in today's lesson we'll be moving out of Middle C Position!

I don't mind moving to a new den...

But moving out of Middle C Position...

Let's show Gary he has nothing to worry about. Place your hands in Middle C Position. Play each piece to the right.

Now, let's move your left hand! In Middle C Position your LH 5 and 4 rest on Bass F and G. Move your hand so that your LH 2 and 1 rest on Bass F and G. Play the pieces again.

Friends In Flight

How will I know where to put my hands when you're not there to help me?

Let's teach Gary how to figure out where to put his hands. In every piano piece, there is a number above or below the first note on each staff. **This finger number** tells you where to place your hands on the piano. Look at the grand staff below.

1. The **3 is above Treble E** on the staff. Place your right-hand fingers on the keys so that your RH 3 is resting on E.

2. The **4 is below Bass G** on the staff. Place your left-hand fingers on the keys so that your LH 4 is resting on G. Look, you're back in Middle C Position . . . but not for long.

Um, Gary? It looks like your balloon is on the move again.

It can't be. I tied it over.... over... Aack!

You better get out there before it's gone. We'll finish up in here with a piano game.

Choose a measure below. Place your hands on the piano according to the finger-number clues. Next, I will point to a note name on Gary's basket. Use your LH to play the corresponding key on the piano. Let's try again!

Can you find notes in the practice pieces below that are stepping up? Can you find notes that are stepping down?

Listen and watch as I play each practice piece. Now it's your turn! Remember to say the note names as you play.

Practice On The Pathway

Can you draw a line from each practice piece to the keyboard image displaying the correct starting position?

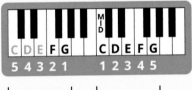

LH   **RH**

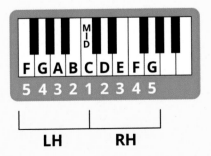

LH   **RH**

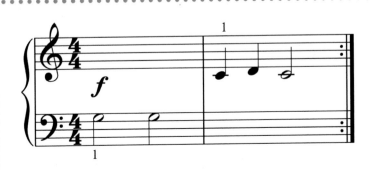

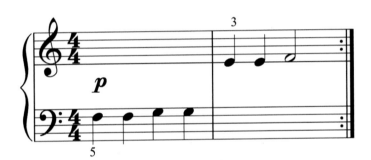

Movin' and Groovin'

Use the finger-number clues to find your starting position.

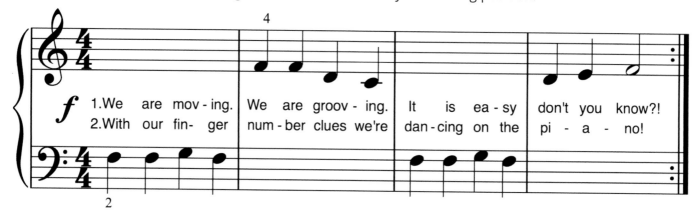

1. We are mov-ing. We are groov-ing. It is ea-sy don't you know?!
2. With our fin-ger num-ber clues we're dan-cing on the pi-a-no!

Floating In My Red Balloon

Use the finger-number clues to find your starting position.

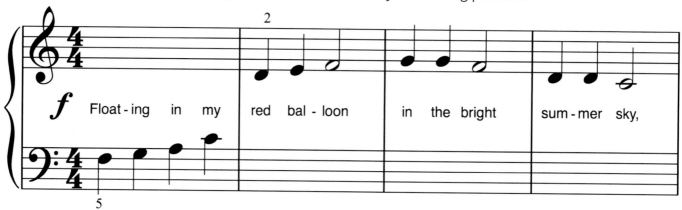

Float-ing in my red bal-loon in the bright sum-mer sky,

I can see my home, sweet home as I'm soar-ing by!

Up, Up And Away

Use the finger-number clues to find your starting position.

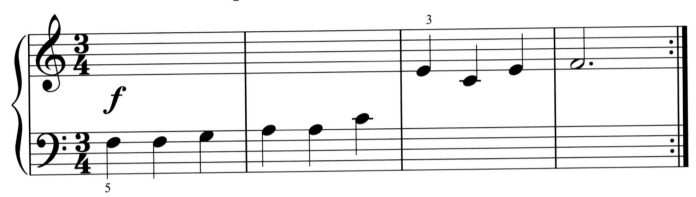

'Round The Town

Use the finger-number clues to find your starting position.

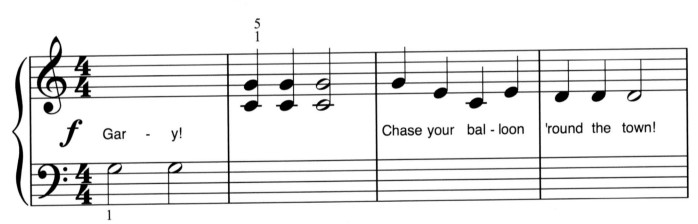

Gar - y!   Chase your bal - loon 'round the town!

Don't   stop   'til it's come back to the ground!

Friends In Flight

Note to Teachers: Welcome to our first *Move And Groove* page. Today your student moved out of Middle C Position for the first time.

While familiar playing positions are useful for beginners, it is helpful to unlock your students from position-based play early and often. *Move And Groove* pages in Primer Books 2 and 3 are included to help with this process.

Move And Groove

1 In today's lesson you moved your left hand to a new starting position. Did you know that **your right hand can move** starting positions, too?

2 In the box above the first measure, write the name of the first note. Next, use the finger-number clue to find the starting position for your right hand. Play the measure while saying the note names.

3 Repeat this procedure for the remaining measures.

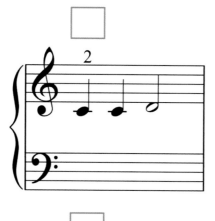

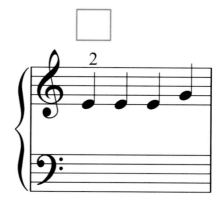

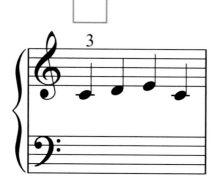

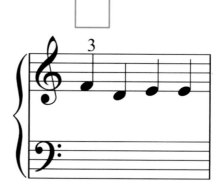

Oh, Sheldon, you look tired.

My friends and I were up all night jamming on the rooftop.

I heard you. I'm feeling a little sleepy myself. But try to keep your eyes open while we learn something new. Sheldon? Sheldon? *Sigh*

Help Me Wake Up Sheldon

zzzzz...

Today we will learn a new note that can't be played with your hands in Middle C Position... so let's practice moving! Choose a grand staff below. Use the finger-number clues to find your starting position. If your hands are in Middle C Position, stay silent. If your hands are not in Middle C Position, press down all the keys to **wake up Sheldon**. Let's play again.

Rooftop Pop

While Sheldon rests, let's learn about Bass C. Bass C is a space note. It is found in the second space on the bass staff. Because it is a low note, its stem points up, but we still play it with your LH. On the piano, place your LH 1 on Bass G. Curve your hand so each finger is resting on its own key. On the piano, Bass C is found below the group of two black keys where your LH 5 is resting. Look at the bass staff below. Practice playing C and G.

Sheldon, wake up! You don't want to miss playing stacked notes with Bass C and G.

Remember stacked notes? Now that you know Bass C, you can play a new set of stacked notes with Bass C and G. With your LH 5 and 1 on C and G, practice playing the stacked notes below.

Did you say stacked nuts?

Oh! Thanks for joining us, Sheldon.

Bye, off to stack some nuts!

Find the stacked notes in the second practice piece. Name the bottom note. Name the top note.

Use your LH 5 to tap all the Bass Cs in the practice pieces.

I will clap a rhythm. Can you point to the practice piece with the matching rhythm?

Practice On The Pathway

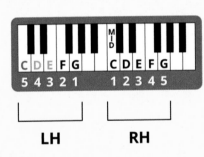

LH   **RH**

Can you find the new dynamic markings in these practice pieces?

mf = *mezzo forte* (medium loud)

mp = *mezzo piano* (medium soft)

Use the finger-number clues to find your starting position and then play each practice piece. Say the note names as you play.

POP

Jammin' On The Rooftop

Use the finger-number clues to find your starting position.

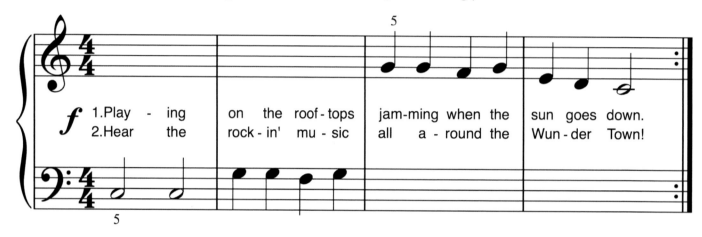

f
1.Play - ing on the roof - tops jam-ming when the sun goes down.
2.Hear the rock - in' mu - sic all a - round the Wun - der Town!

Wake Up, Sleepy Head

Use the finger-number clues to find your starting position.

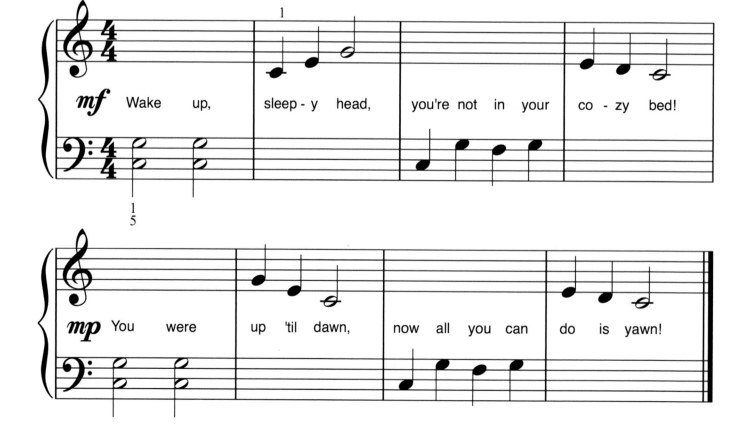

mf Wake up, sleep - y head, you're not in your co - zy bed!

mp You were up 'til dawn, now all you can do is yawn!

Game Instructions

Note: The playing cards for *Rooftop Pop* are found at the end of this book.

Players: two players

Materials: one laminated game board, twelve coins, two dice, ten playing cards

Game Objectives:

Musical Objective: To reinforce recognition of Cs on the grand staff
Game Objective: To wake up the neighbors

Setting It Up:

Players should sit beside one another with the deck of cards placed between. Each player should have a die. Six coins should be placed over six windows (one per window) on the game board.

How To Play:

1. To begin, one player removes the top card from the deck and flips it over to reveal an image of notes on the grand staff.

2. At this point, the game becomes a race. While explained for Player 1 only, both players will perform Step 3 (below) simultaneously.

3. As soon as the card in Step 1 is revealed, Player 1 determines the number of Cs on the grand staff and then attempts to roll the corresponding number on her die.

4. The first player to roll the correct number on her die wins the round. If the winner is the student, a coin is placed over a window image on the game board for each C on the grand staff. For example, if two Cs were on the grand staff, two windows are covered with coins. If the winner is the teacher, a coin is removed from a window for each C on the grand staff.

5. Players repeat Steps 1 to 4 until every window is covered with a coin (the student wins), every coin is removed from every window (the teachers wins), or all cards are removed from the deck.

6. If all cards have been removed from the deck, players count the number of coins on the game board. If there are six or fewer coins on the game board, the teacher wins. If there are more than six coins on the game board, the student wins.

Ruby, I didn't know you lived on a farm.

I don't, but I do have to round up my cousins.

You're a busy bunny, but your roundup is going to have to wait. Leave your boots by the door and join us as we learn to find a new D.

D On The Bass Staff

1. **Bass D is a line note** that sits on the middle line of the bass staff. On the keyboard, D is one step above Bass C.

2. Listen as I clap a simple rhythm. Can you play the rhythm back on Bass C? D?

3. Look at the measure of music to the right. Use the finger-number clue to find your starting position. Practice stepping between C and D.

There's a bunny.

Where's my lasso?

5

Skipping Between Bass D And Bass F

While Ruby rounds up her cousin, let's skip between Bass D and F.

D and F are both line notes. This means that **we can skip** between D and F. Look at the music below. Find the places that 1) skip up, 2) skip down and 3) repeat. Use the finger-number clue to find your starting position. Say the note names as you play.

Is that a baby bunny under my piano bench?

Whoops. Time to round 'em up again!

They sure keep you busy! But before you gallop off, join us as we round up some Ds.

So long, partner.

Let's help Ruby round up some Bass Ds. Look at the measures of music below. Draw a line from each measure containing a D to Ruby's lasso. Now play each measure.

Can you find notes in the practice pieces below that are skipping up? Skipping down?

Use your LH 4 to tap all the Bass Ds. Use your LH 5 to tap all the Bass Cs.

Find your starting position for the first piece. I will point to a note. Play its matching key.

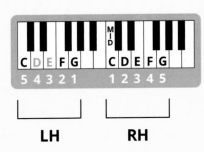

LH   **RH**

Listen as I clap the rhythms of the practice pieces. Can you clap the rhythms back to me?

Use the finger-number clues to find your starting position and then play each practice piece. Say the note names as you play.

Did you remember to play the second practice piece *mezzo piano*? Did you remember to play the third practice piece *mezzo forte*?

Rabbit Rodeo

Use the finger-number clues to find your starting position.

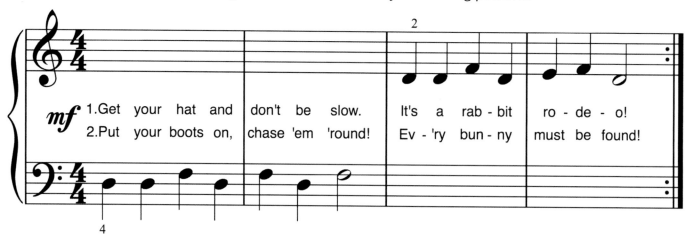

1. Get your hat and don't be slow. It's a rab-bit ro-de-o!
2. Put your boots on, chase 'em 'round! Ev-'ry bun-ny must be found!

Home By Four

Use the finger-number clues
to find your starting position.

Round 'em up and out the door. Get those bun-nies home by four!

Keep 'em in a nice straight line. This cow-bun-ny's do-ing fine!

Middle C Memories

Use the finger-number clues to find your starting position.

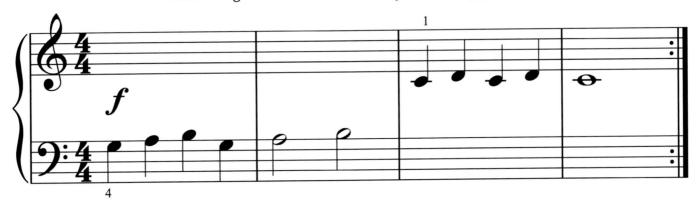

The Cowbunny's Campfire

Use the finger number clues to find your starting position.

Note: When using the teacher duet, the student part is played one octave higher than written.

Rabbit Rancher

1 Are you ready to **Move And Groove?**

2 In the box above the first measure, write the name of the first note. Next, use the finger-number clue to find the starting position for your hand. Play the piece while saying the note names.

3 Repeat this procedure for the remaining pieces.

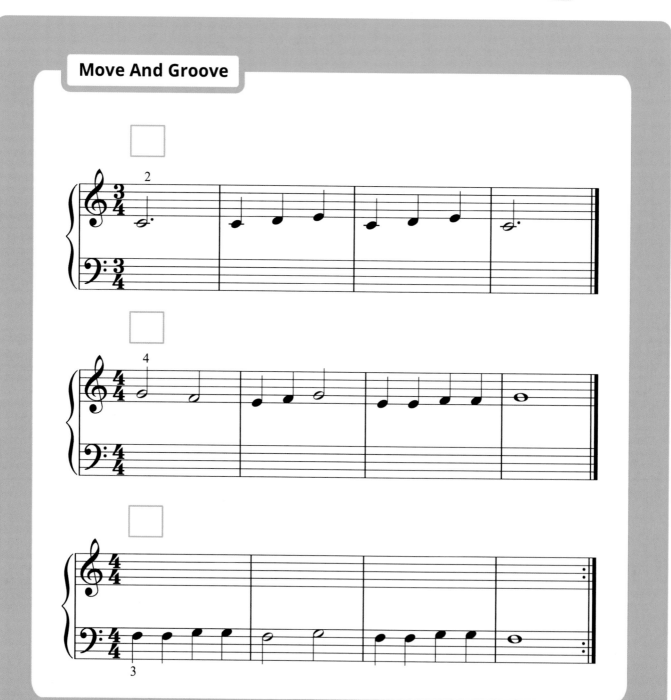

Move And Groove

You made some nice saves today, Maxine.

Gulp! I just closed my eyes and hoped for the best.

It worked! No one could find an open space in that net! Speaking of spaces, come join us as we learn a new space note.

This will be easier with your eyes open.

E On The Bass Staff

1. **Bass E is a space note** that sits in the third space of the bass staff. On the keyboard, E is a step higher than D.

2. Listen as I clap a simple rhythm. Can you play the rhythm back on Bass D? E? C?

3. Look at the measure of music to the right. Use the finger-number clue to find your starting position and then practice stepping **between C, D, and E.**

5

Soccer Ball Storm

While Maxine works up the courage to open her eyes, let's **skip on Bass C, E, and G.**

Bass C, E, and G are all space notes. This means we can skip between them. In the music below, can you point to all the Es? The Cs? The Gs? Next, find your starting position and play the piece.

> No thanks! Black and white keys remind me of black and white soccer balls.

> Maxine, what on earth are you wearing?

> Gary's scuba mask! Now I'm safe from soccer balls.

> Do you really need the snorkel? Never mind. Let's play a soccer game with the C 5-Finger Scale.

The C 5-Finger Scale

> My team is meeting for pizza. I have to get there before Gary. Bye!

Place your LH 5, 4, 3, 2, and 1 on Bass C, D, E, F, and G. If I point to a soccer ball with an arrow pointing up, play and say, "C-D-E-F-G." If I point to a soccer ball with an arrow pointing down, play and say, "G-F-E-D-C." Let's play again with your RH 1, 2, 3, 4, and 5 on Middle C, D, E, F, and G.

 C-D-E-F-G ➤ G-F-E-D-C ➤ C-D-E-F-G ➤ G-F-E-D-C ➤

Can you find notes in the practice pieces below that are skipping up? Skipping down?

Use your LH 3 to tap all the Bass Es. Use your LH 4 to tap all the Bass Ds.

Find your starting position for the first piece. I will point to a note. Play its matching key.

Practice On The Pathway

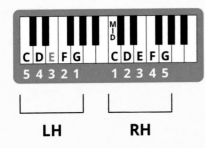

LH   RH

Listen as I clap the rhythms of the practice pieces. Can you clap the rhythms back to me?

Use the finger-number clues to find your **starting position** and then play each practice piece. Say the note names as you play.

Did you remember to play the first practice piece medium soft? Did you remember to play the second practice piece medium loud?

Hat Trick

Use the finger-number clues to find your starting position.

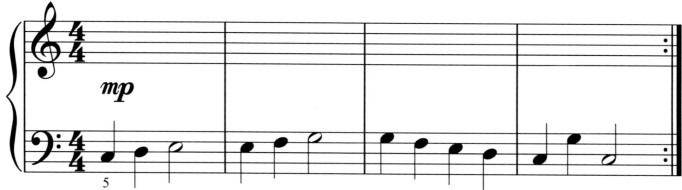

Kick To Win

Use the finger-number clues to find your starting position.

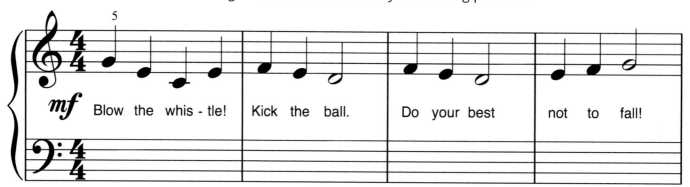

Blow the whis - tle! | Kick the ball. | Do your best | not to fall!

Pass to Max - ine; | call her name! | Try to win the | soc - cer game!

Note: When using the teacher duet, the student part is played one octave higher than written.

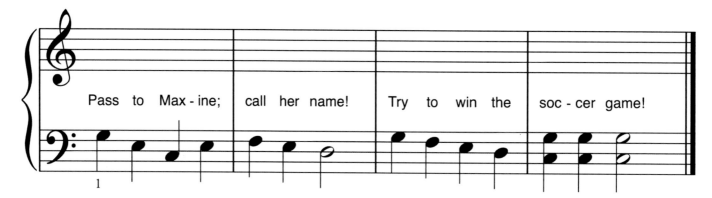

R.H.
L.H.

Eye On The Ball

Use the finger-number clues to find your starting position.

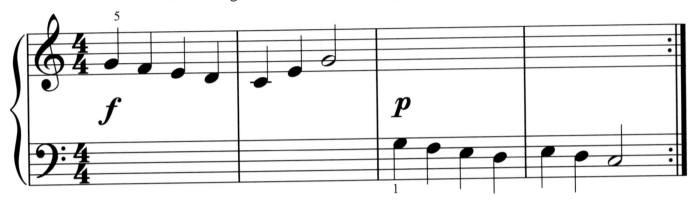

Playing For Pizza

Use the finger-number clues to find your starting position.

Let's all go for piz - za right a - fter we play!

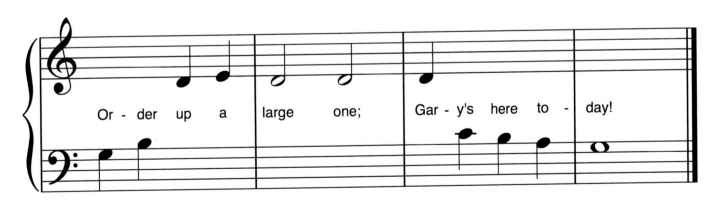

Or - der up a large one; Gar - y's here to - day!

 Soccer Ball Storm

Offside

Use the finger-number clues to find your starting position.

mp

3

Soccer Ball Storm

Use the finger-number clues to find your starting position.

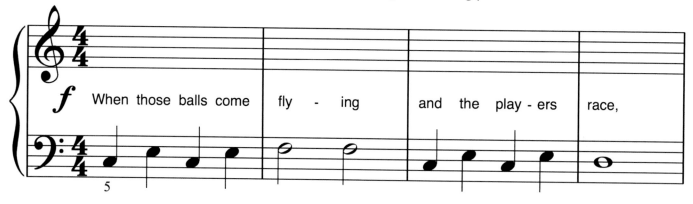

f When those balls come | fly - ing | and the play - ers | race,

5

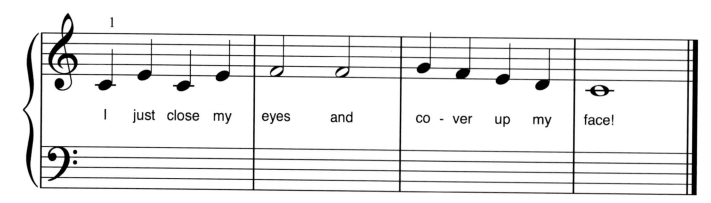

1

I just close my | eyes and | co - ver up my | face!

 Storm

Note: The playing cards for *Soccer Ball Storm* are found at the end of this book.

Players: two players   **Materials:** one laminated game board, three pennies, three dimes, two dice, five playing cards

Game Objectives:

Musical Objective: To reinforce recognition of notes on the bass staff
Game Objective: To place coins over more soccer balls than an opposing player

Setting It Up:

Players should sit beside one another with the deck of cards placed between. Each player should have a die. Player 1 should have three pennies. Player 2 should have three dimes.

How To Play:

1. To begin, one player removes the top card from the deck and flips it over to reveal an image of three notes on the bass staff.

2. At this point, the game becomes a race. While explained for Player 1 only, both players will perform Step 3 (below) simultaneously.

3. As soon as the card in Step 1 is revealed, Player 1 determines the names of the notes on the bass staff and then attempts to roll a number on her die that matches the number on the soccer ball image on the game board that displays the three matching note names.

4. The first player to roll the correct number on her die wins the round. The player winning the round uses a coin to cover the soccer ball with the note names matching the note images displayed on the card revealed in Step 1.

5. Players repeat Steps 1 to 4 until all soccer ball images on the game board have been covered with coins.

6. At this point the game is over and the player with the most coins on the game board wins the game.

Cut and laminate the card sets below.

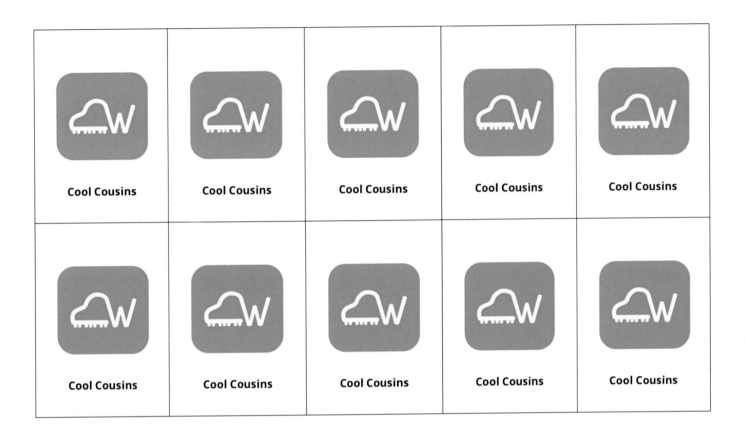

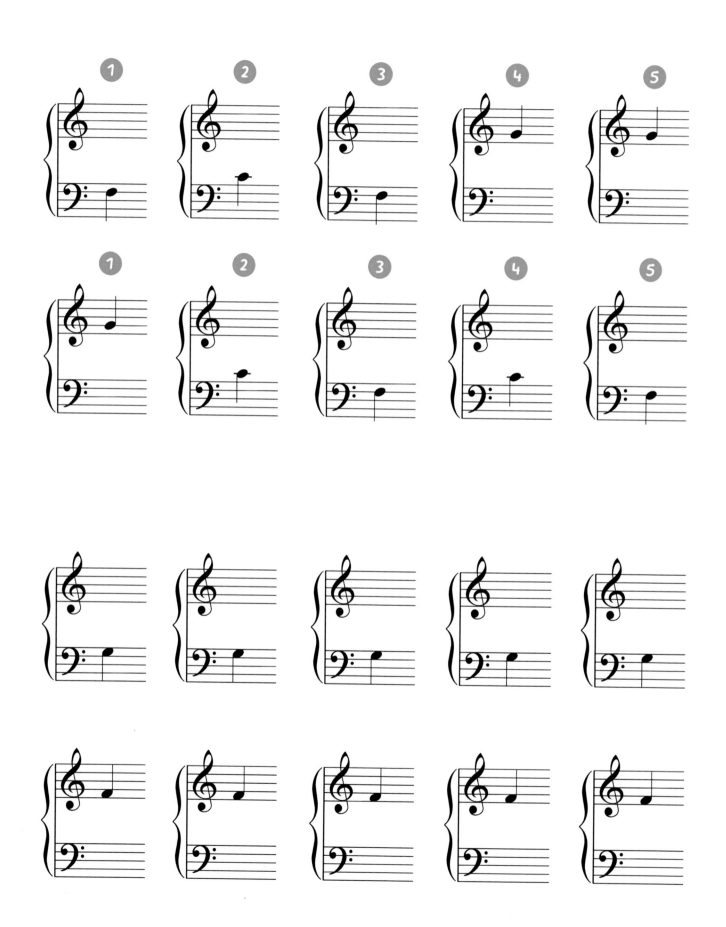

Cut and laminate the card sets below.

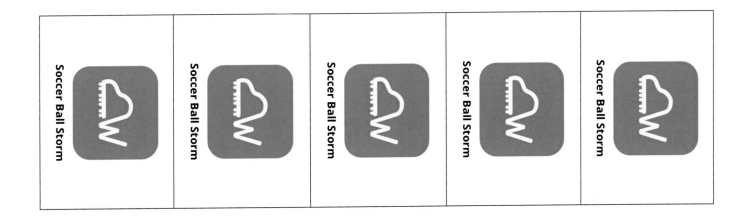

Rooftop Pop

Rooftop Pop

Rooftop Pop

Rooftop Pop

Rooftop Pop

Rooftop Pop

Rooftop Pop

Rooftop Pop

Rooftop Pop

Rooftop Pop

Soccer Ball Storm

Soccer Ball Storm

Soccer Ball Storm

Soccer Ball Storm

Soccer Ball Storm

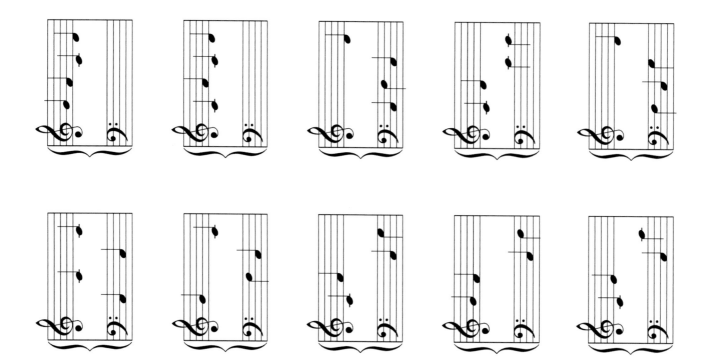

 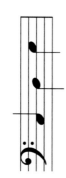  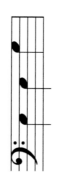 

Certificate of Completion

has completed WunderKeys Primer Piano Book Two

HIP HIP HOORAY!

Made in the USA
Monee, IL
16 June 2024

59886991R00038